# Dad Jokes Christmas Gift Book

by Ralph Lane

Thank you for selecting a Ralph Lane book. Ralph's gift books make great gifts for birthdays, holidays, gift baskets, stocking stuffers, bathroom books, vacation books or just for the fun of it. Please consider leaving a review for this book on amazon.com  or goodreads.com. And don't forget to suggest Ralph Lane books to your friends and family. If you enjoy this book, you'll also love the original *Dad Jokes Gift Book* by Ralph Lane.

# Table of Contents

# Christmas Carol Comedy

Note on door: "Dear Christmas Carolers: The only thing that can bring **Joy To The World** is a **Silent Night**."

Who is a Christmas tree's favorite singer?

**Spruce Springsteen**

How is the alphabet different on Christmas than any other day?

**On Christmas, it has Noel.**

**Who is their favorite singer at the North Pole?**

Elfish Presley

What song do monkeys sing at Christmas?

**Jungle Bells**

3

# The Lighter Side of Santa's Elves

What do they learn at
the North Pole
Elementary
School?

A B C D E F G
H I J K L M N
O P Q R S T U
V W X Y Z ? ?

**The elf-a-bet**

If athletes get athlete's foot,
what do elves get?

**Mistle-toes**

What do you English teachers
call Santa's elves?

**Subordinate
Clauses**

Why was
Santa's little
helper
depressed?

**Because she had
low elf esteem.**

What is
green, white
and red all
over?

**A sunburned elf**

# Holly Jolly Holidays

What I don't like about office Christmas parties is looking for a new job the next day.

How did Scrooge win the football game?

**The ghost of Christmas passed.**

What do you get if you eat Christmas tree decorations?

**Tinselitis**

This holiday season, in lieu of gifts, I've decided to give everyone...

... my opinion!!

What did Adam say on the day before Christmas?

It's Christmas, Eve!

Why is it always
cold at
Christmas?

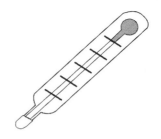

**Because it's in
Decembrrrrr.**

Where does
Christmas come
before Thanksgiving?

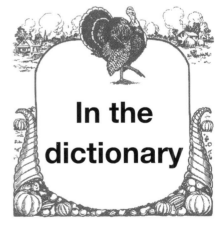

**In the
dictionary**

Never catch
snowflakes on
your tongue...

...until all the birds
have gone south for
the winter!

Why is
Christmas just
like your job?

You do all the work and
the fat guy with the suit
gets all the credit!

At Christmas time, there's nothing I love more than sitting in front of a warm fire, mulled wine in hand and singing Christmas songs until I slowly fall asleep.

**Maybe that's why I'm no longer a fireman.**

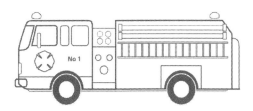

# Reindeer and Other Christmas Critters

Most people don't realize that Santa had a dozen reindeer. Of course there's Dasher, Dancer, Prancer, Vixen, Comet, Cupid, Donner, Blitzen and Rudolph. That makes nine. Then there's Olive as in "Olive the other reindeer." And we all know about Howe because the song clearly reminds us "Howe all the reindeer loved him…" And finally there's good old Andy who we are told, "Andy shouted out with glee." That makes twelve.

Why did Ebenezer Scrooge keep a pet lamb?

**Because he loved to hear it say, "Baaaaahh humbug!"**

What do you call a shark that delivers toys at Christmas?

**Santa Jaws!**

What do
sheep say to
each other at
Christmas?

**Merry Christmas
to ewe.**

 Who delivers
Christmas
presents to dogs?

**Santa Paws**

Why didn't
Rudolph get
a good
report card?

**Because he went down in History.**

What do you
call an impolite
reindeer?

**RUDEolph**

# Did you know Santa only had eight reindeer last Christmas?

## Comet stayed home to clean the sink.

# Santa Jokes

What did Santa say when he woke on Christmas morning to find the *Dad Jokes Christmas Gift Book* in his stocking?

**It's the best gift I've ever gotten!! But next time could you put it in a stocking I'm not wearing?**

What do you call a Santa who's afraid of going down the chimney on Christmas Eve?

**Claustrophobic**

What do you call a kid who doesn't believe in Santa?

**A rebel without a Claus**

What do you call
Santa living at
the South Pole?

**A lost clause**

What does Santa bring naughty
boys and girls on Christmas Eve?

**A pack of batteries with a note
saying, "Toy not included"**

What nationality
is Santa Claus?

Santa and Rudolph
at the North Pole

**North Polish**

Ho! Ho! Ho!

Merry Christmas!

What goes
"oh oh oh"?

**Santa walking
backwards**

Where does santa keep his money?

in a snow bank

How much did Santa pay for his sleigh?

**It was on the house!**

What does
Santa do in
his garden?

**He hoe hoe hoes.**

What do you call
Santa Claus when
he doesn't move?

**Santa Pause**

An honest politician, a kind lawyer and Santa Claus were talking when they all noticed a $5 bill on the floor. Who picked it up?

**Santa of course; the other two are fictional characters.**

What do you call a man who claps at Christmas?

**Santapplause**

What kind of
motorcycle does
Santa ride?

**A Holly
Davidson**

What is Santa's
favorite place to
deliver presents?

**Idaho-ho-ho**

# Snowman Jokes

What do snowmen
eat for breakfast?

**Ice Crispies and
Frosted Snow Flakes**

What do you get
when you cross
a snowman with
a vampire?

**Frostbite**

If we call him *Frosty the Snowman* in December, what do we call him in May?

**A puddle**

What does *Frosty the Snowman* take when he gets sick?

*A chill pill*

Where does a
snowman keep
his money?

**In a snow
bank**

What do you call a
female snowman?

*A snow-ma'am*

# What does a snow-ma'am put on her face at night?

## cold cream

What did one snowman say to the other?

## Do you smell carrots?

What do snowman
beatniks say to
each other?

You're cool.

What do you
call a snowman
party?

A Snowball

Why did the snow
man turn yellow?

**Ask the dog.**

What did the police
officer say when he
saw a snowman
committing a crime?

**Freeze!!**

Made in the USA
Middletown, DE
29 November 2019